THE GOURMET
SLOW COOKER

VOLUME II

─◦ THE GOURMET ◦─
SLOW COOKER

VOLUME II

Regional Comfort-Food Classics

Lynn Alley

PHOTOGRAPHY BY

Leo Gong

TEN SPEED PRESS
Berkeley | Toronto

Ten Speed Press
PO Box 7123
Berkeley, California 94707
www.tenspeed.com

Distributed in Australia by Simon and Schuster Australia,
in Canada by Ten Speed Press Canada, in New Zealand by
Southern Publishers Group, in South Africa by Real Books, and
in the United Kingdom and Europe by Publishers Group UK.

Cover and text design by Catherine Jacobes
Food styling by Karen Shinto
Food styling assistance by Jeff Larsen
Prop styling by Natalie Hoelen
Photography assistance by Harumi Shimizu

Library of Congress Cataloging-in-Publication Data
Alley, Lynn.
    The gourmet slow cooker volume II : regional comfort-food
classics / Lynn Alley.
        p. cm.
Includes index.
    ISBN-13: 978-1-58008-732-2 (pbk.)
    ISBN-10: 1-58008-732-9 (pbk.)
1. Casserole cookery. 2. Cookery, International. I. Title.
TX693.A446 2003
641.8'21—dc21   2003006074

First printing, 2006
Printed in China

1 2 3 4 5 6 7 8 9 10 — 10 09 08 07 06

To M., as always, with love and gratitude

CONTENTS

Acknowledgments

Thanks to all my friends and neighbors who willingly and enthusiastically ate my food and gave me their critical feedback. Neighbors Helen Mildner, Ernie and Bob Tassoni, Marie Pike, and Rosella Heffner were ever at-the-ready with knife and fork. Gratitude also to the staff at the Chopra Center in Carlsbad (D. G., Monica, Anastacia, Leili, Caeli, Amanda, Ben, Mel, Tim, Travis, Hari, Asha, Max, Jennifer, Alisha, Lorri, Samara, Neil, and Brooke), for their enthusiastic appetites and candid, useful comments.

And, of course, Laddie, my Bouvier, faithfully performed his duties as curator of trash. He has been assisted, though decidedly more selectively, by Crystal, my eighteen-year-old Himalayan kitty.

To my friend, talented cook, and author Beth Hensperger, who is always ready to share advice, gossip, recipes, and immoral support. Special thanks to Brooke Myers for recipe testing and feedback.

To the crew at Ten Speed Press for total backup, as always. To Phil Wood, my constant supporter; Lorena Jones, who always has good ideas and ready comments; Lily Binns, my editor, for her patient guidance and work and her kindness, courtesy, and flexibility in accommodating my schedule; Mark Anderson, Dennis Hayes, and the sales crew for selling my books; Kristin Casemore in publicity; and never let me forget Kristine Standley, who cuts the checks and makes my day!

Thanks to the following company representatives who donated both equipment and advice to the effort: Melissa Palmer at All-Clad, Mary Rodgers at Cuisinart, and Heather Scherman at Porter Novelli for Braun.

And to Margaret Zink, for being my mom and friend.

Introduction

The recipes in this book, while far from exhaustive, have been chosen to celebrate some of the culinary, agricultural, and cultural influences I have most enjoyed as I've lived and traveled all over this country. They are all inspired by regional heritages created by generations of immigrants and native peoples. The foods of the southwestern United States, for example, are richly layered blends of flavors that come from both European and Native American traditions, culminating in slow-cooked dishes like chili, posole, and a variety of stews. Through much experimentation, I've learned that barbecue dishes from the South and Midwest work surprisingly well in a slow cooker, as do New England chowders and breads. The slow cooker is perfect for fruit preserves and desserts—the longer and slower they cook, the sweeter they become—and even high-end chocolate has its place over this kind of gentle heat. The slow cooker is clearly a bottomless pot when it comes to adapting favorite recipes to the lifestyle of the busy but discerning home cook.

We now live in a land of abundance such as has been experienced by few people in history, with access to a wide variety of organic produce, sustainably raised meat, and specialty products unlike anything we've experienced before. Good ingredients make a difference in both nutrition and flavor, and there's no reason we shouldn't use them in the slow cooker. Not all of the recipes found in this book are traditional, but they take inspiration, as did the recipes of our forefathers, from the wealth of good ingredients and the richness of local traditions found in all corners of our country. I hope that some among them will become traditions in your home.

Choosing a Slow Cooker

For my first book on slow cooking, *The Gourmet Slow Cooker,* I tested all the recipes in machines I could then afford: the $19.99 specials from Home Depot and Target. I figured one slow cooker was as good as the next.

I had two or three different brands in two or three different sizes. I'd test one recipe in the Hamilton Beach, another in the General Electric, and a third in the Rival. It never occurred to me to test one recipe in three different brands of slow cooker.

Not, that is, until a reader wrote in saying that she followed my instructions for cooking beef burgundy to the letter, but that the liquid was completely gone by the specified end time. My editor asked me to retest the recipe to see if any change needed to be made in the amount of liquid called for. I tested it again and found that the suggested cooking time

and the amount of liquid worked perfectly. I wondered what had gone wrong, and then it began to dawn on me that the fault might lie with the slow cooker.

Different slow cookers cook at different temperatures. One manufacturer's low temperature may not be the same as another's. In general, the low setting should fall between 180°F and 200°F, and a high setting generally cooks around a hundred degrees higher. Cooking temperatures will vary depending on the size of the cooker, the altitude of the kitchen, the density and temperature of the food before it is placed in the crock, and how full the crock is filled. Knowing your slow cooker's range in temperature is useful when cooking large pieces of meat, such as a pork loin (which should hit 165°F) or turkey breast (175°F), and other meats which must be cooked to a specific temperature in order to ensure safety. If you want to assess your cooking temperatures, use a kitchen thermometer and insert it into the middle of the contents of the crock, without letting it touch the bottom, or in the case of meat, the bone, two or three hours into the cooking time. With meat, the thermometer should be inserted into the center.

So the one caveat I dish out with this book is "get to know your own slow cooker" and carefully observe how it cooks. Cooking times may vary according to manufacturer, model, and even, I am told, the amount of power coming into your house at any given time or in any given area.

You may also find that the less expensive cookers have hot spots around the edges, while every effort has been made to stabilize the heat in the more expensive models. This may not matter much with the majority of recipes, but it is still a good idea to give the contents of your cooker a stir now and again. When baking cakes in the cooker, you may wish to carefully lift out the insert with potholders, turn it around, and then reinsert it for more even baking. You can certainly prepare your meals with an inexpensive slow cooker; I have cooked many good ones in mine. Just be aware of its possible shortcomings and idiosyncrasies. Watch it closely at first until you have a good sense of its timing.

You may also wish to consider the different sizes and shapes available in slow cookers. The tiniest crock I have found, one and a half quarts, is perfect for cooking for one, and for making appetizers and dips. The four- to five-quart pots are good for families of four, and the seven-quart models are necessary for entertaining. Round pots are good for soups, grains, and bean dishes, but in general, the oval shape is more practical, as it accommodates large pieces of meat, and gives more surface area and visibility.

A few other things to take into consideration when buying a slow cooker: Is the instruction book comprehensive and informative? Does the enclosed recipe book have good ideas and clear instructions? Is there a customer service number listed? If so, be sure to save it.

The following is a list of some of the more reliable slow cooker manufacturers:

All-Clad	Kuhn Rikon
Breville	Proctor-Silex
CorningWare	Rival
Cuisinart	Russell Hobbs
EuroPro	West Bend
Farberware	
General Electric	
Hamilton Beach	

Tips for Using a Slow Cooker

Fill the slow cooker no more than two-thirds full. The food just doesn't cook properly if the container is filled to the top.

The optimum temperature for obtaining tender meat is around 180°F, which is the low setting on most slow cookers. As temperatures rise, protein fibers begin to constrict and toughen, so in general you don't want to cook meats on the high setting.

Having said that, I hasten to add that **you should never try to cook on the warm setting,** which falls below 140°F. The temperature is just too low for food safety. Once it is cooked, food can generally be held safely on the warm setting for up to 4 hours.

To ensure even and thorough cooking, always be sure that meat and other foods are completely defrosted before consigning them to a slow cooker.

Adding frozen foods to the cooker will lengthen your cooking time considerably.

To thicken foods in the slow cooker, you can use one of these three methods:

- Stir 1 or 2 tablespoons of cornstarch into the cooking liquid before you add it to the pot.

- Add 1 or 2 tablespoons of Gold Medal's Wondra quick-mixing flour to the sauce and stir in thoroughly. Wondra is designed to easily incorporate into liquids without clumping.

- Add 2 or 3 tablespoons of rice to anything you plan to purée before serving.

Browning meats and veggies before adding them to your dish will always add extra dimensions of flavor. Although it's not a necessary step in making a good stew, browning begins caramelization, breaks down cell walls, releases flavors, and extracts fat-soluble components from the ingredients.

To keep them fresh and aromatic, add tender vegetables and herbs to your dish during the last twenty to thirty minutes of cooking time.

Contrary to what many slow cooker manuals will tell you, I suggest you **lift the lid,** smelling, tasting, and poking the food around. What kind of cook wouldn't? It may throw your cooking time off by up to 15 minutes or so, but the slow cooker is designed for flexibility and forgiveness.

To save time, do the prep work the night before, store the various ingredients in separate containers in the refrigerator, then arrange them in the slow cooker before you leave the house in the morning.

Always refrigerate leftovers within an hour or two after cooking to prevent the growth of dangerous bacteria.

Your slow cooker uses about the same amount of electricity as a 75-watt light bulb, much less than either a conventional gas or electric oven. And it won't heat up your kitchen in warm weather. Relaxing over a slow cooker is better than slaving over a hot stove any day.

Useful Equipment

There are only a few pieces of kitchen equipment that I find indispensable when I am using the slow cooker.

- I used to suggest puréeing slow-cooked soups in batches in a conventional blender. What a mess. Then I discovered the handheld blender. You plug it in, insert the blender end into the slow cooker, being careful not to touch the insides of the interior, and gently move it around until everything has been neatly puréed. I would never go without one now.

- Silicon spatulas are essential for stirring the contents of a slow cooker without scratching the interior.

- A plastic whisk is also a good investment, again to avoid scratching the interior of the slow cooker.

- A simple probe thermometer is good for testing the temperature of meat and for getting to know your slow cooker's overall temperature range.

- Good spoon rests are a must. Get one and park it right next to the cooker.

- A good food processor can be helpful for chopping and other prep work.

- Some nice, cushy potholders will be helpful for lifting the hot inserts out of the casings.

- And, of course, a glass of wine or cold microbrew for the cook while he or she works.

Soups, Chilis & Stews

Santa Fe Sweet Potato Soup / 10

Potato-Cilantro Bisque / 12

Black Bean–Chicken Chili / 13

Cream of Castroville Artichoke Soup / 14

Gilroy Garlic Soup / 15

Green Posole / 16

Three Sisters Stew / 18

Brunswick Stew / 19

Chicken and Seafood Gumbo / 20

Peanut Soup / 21

White Bean Chili / 22

Redeye Stew / 24

Salmon, Mushroom, Sorrel, and Aromatic Rice Bisque / 25

Tillamook Cheddar and Beer Soup / 26

Walla Walla Onion Soup / 27

San Francisco Cioppino / 28

Butternut Squash and Apple Soup / 30

Clam and Potato Chowder / 31

Iowa Corn Chowder / 32

Roasted Carrot-Parsnip Soup / 33

SANTA FE SWEET POTATO SOUP

⤳ Serves 4 ⤳

The sweet potatoes in this comforting soup need nothing more than traditional Southwestern spices and a topping of jalapeños and toasted pepitas *(pumpkin seeds).*

Place a large sauté pan over medium heat and add the oil. Add the onion and sauté for about 10 minutes, until lightly browned. Add the sweet potatoes and garlic and continue cooking for 10 minutes, until they begin to brown.

Transfer the contents of the pan to the slow cooker and add the water. Cover and cook on low for about 6 hours, until the sweet potatoes are quite tender when pierced with a fork. Coarsely grind the oregano, chili powder, cinnamon, cloves, and allspice in a coffee mill or using mortar and pestle and add to the soup. Continue cooking for 1 hour. Using a handheld blender, gently purée the soup until smooth. Season to taste with salt.

Ladle into bowls and serve hot, topped with a few slices of jalapeño, a sprinkling of toasted *pepitas,* and a dollop of crème fraîche.

SUGGESTED BEVERAGE: A spicy white wine is in order here, something along the lines of a Cortese, Dry Creek Vineyard's Chenin Blanc, or a Gewürztraminer.

1 tablespoon pumpkin seed oil or other vegetable oil

1 yellow onion, chopped

2 sweet potatoes, peeled, cut into chunks

4 cloves garlic, whole

6 to 8 cups chicken stock (page 91) or water

1 teaspoon dried oregano

1 tablespoon chili powder

1 cinnamon stick

6 whole cloves

10 allspice berries

Salt

2 jalapeño chiles, stemmed, seeded, and julienned, for garnish

1/4 cup toasted *pepitas,* chopped, for garnish

1/2 cup crème fraîche or sour cream, for garnish

POTATO-CILANTRO BISQUE

~ Serves 4 ~

This comforting soup is delicately spiced with classic flavors and ingredients of the Southwest.

Place the potatoes, stock, and garlic in the slow cooker. Cover and cook on low for about 4 hours, until the potatoes are tender when pierced with a fork. Using a handheld blender, carefully purée the potatoes and garlic until smooth.

Grind the coriander and cumin seeds in a coffee mill or using a mortar and pestle and add to the soup. Add the chiles, green onions, cilantro, sour cream, and salt to taste and stir well. Continue cooking for 1 hour. Ladle into bowls and serve at once.

SUGGESTED BEVERAGE: Mount Palomar Winery in Temecula, California, makes the only Cortese (a northern Italian white wine grape variety) in the United States, as far as I know. Winemaker Etienne Cowper discovered Cortese vines in an abandoned vineyard in New Mexico and moved cuttings to a vineyard in Temecula. It's a crisp, delightful wine and goes beautifully with this soup.

4 large russet potatoes, peeled and quartered

6 cups chicken stock (page 91) or water

3 cloves garlic, whole

1 teaspoon coriander seeds

1 teaspoon cumin seeds

1 (4-ounce) can diced roasted green chiles

1 bunch green onions, green parts only, thinly sliced

1/2 cup cilantro leaves, coarsely chopped

1 cup sour cream

Salt

BLACK BEAN—CHICKEN CHILI

—◦ Serves 4 ◦—

Black beans work so well in the slow cooker that they seem to be made for it. Grilling the onions and chiles adds an extra dimension of flavor to this dish, which can also be made without the chicken for a vegetarian version. This dish is best made one day ahead, then reheated and served when the flavors have had a chance to meld.

Preheat the broiler. Place the onion, garlic, poblanos, and jalapeños on a baking sheet, with the chiles skin side up. Place under the broiler and grill for about 10 minutes, until the onion and garlic are quite soft and the chile skins are blackened. Cover the chiles with a damp kitchen towel and let rest for about 20 minutes. Peel off the skins or scrape them off using a paring knife. Remove the stems and seeds. Coarsely chop the chiles, garlic, and onion.

Grind the cumin and coriander seeds in a coffee mill or with a mortar and pestle.

Drain the beans and place them in the slow cooker. Add the chiles, garlic, onion, ground spices, water, tomatoes, chili powder, and oregano. Cover and cook on low for 6 hours. Add the beer, cocoa powder, and chicken and continue cooking on low for 2 hours, until the meat is very tender. (In a pinch, you could put all the ingredients in the pot at the same time and cook for 6 to 8 hours. By adding the chicken during the last 2 hours, you will retain some of the chunks.) Season to taste with salt and pepper. Serve at once.

VARIATIONS: Use 6 chicken legs or 10 drumsticks rather than the cubed chicken breast. Add chorizo sausage for additional flavor.

SUGGESTED BEVERAGE: The town of Tecate is famous for its brewery and its numerous fine brews. A Tecate beer would be great with your chili.

1 large yellow onion, peeled, quartered

5 cloves garlic, peeled

2 green poblano chiles, halved

2 jalapeño chiles, halved

1 tablespoon cumin seeds

1 tablespoon coriander seeds

2 cups dried black beans, rinsed and soaked overnight

6 cups chicken stock (page 91) or water

1 (16-ounce) can crushed tomatoes, undrained

3 tablespoons chili powder

2 tablespoons dried Mexican oregano

1 cup beer

$1/4$ cup unsweetened cocoa powder

4 boneless skinless chicken breasts, cubed

Salt and freshly ground black pepper

$1/2$ cup grated Monterey Jack or cheddar cheese, for garnish

$1/2$ cup sour cream, for garnish

Cream of Castroville Artichoke Soup

—⟋ Serves 4 ⟍—

Castroville, California (population 6,724 as of the 2000 census), is the self-proclaimed Artichoke Center of the World. About 75 percent of the state's artichokes are grown there. In 1947, young Norma Jean Baker (later known as Marilyn Monroe) was crowned Castroville's first "artichoke queen." And as you might imagine, the local residents have invented a plethora of artichoke-based foods, this creamy soup not the least among them.

Combine the flour, salt, and thyme in a resealable plastic bag. Add the artichoke hearts and shake until evenly coated.

Place a large sauté pan over medium high heat and add the oil and butter. In batches if necessary, add the artichoke hearts and sauté, stirring occasionally, for 15 minutes, until golden brown on all sides. Add the onion and garlic and cook for another 5 minutes, until softened.

Transfer the contents of the pan to the slow cooker and add the rice and stock. Cover and cook on low for 5 to 6 hours, until the rice is quite tender. Using a handheld blender, purée the soup until smooth. Stir in the whipping cream and lemon juice and season with salt to taste.

Ladle the soup into individual bowls and garnish with the tarragon and a dollop of sour cream. Serve immediately.

SUGGESTED BEVERAGE: Though artichokes are considered a difficult match for most wines, a crisp, dry white wine or a hearty beer would work here.

Ingredients

- $1/2$ cup all-purpose flour
- 2 teaspoons salt
- $1/8$ teaspoon dried thyme
- 2 (12-ounce) packages frozen artichoke hearts, thawed
- 2 tablespoons olive oil
- 1 tablespoon unsalted butter
- 1 yellow onion, coarsely chopped
- 2 cloves garlic, pressed
- $1/4$ cup uncooked converted rice
- 5 cups chicken stock (page 91)
- 1 cup heavy whipping cream or half-and-half
- Dash of freshly squeezed lemon juice or dry white wine
- Salt
- Several sprigs of tarragon, for garnish
- Sour cream, for garnish

GILROY GARLIC SOUP

—ơ Serves 4 ơ—

Located in California's San Joaquin Valley, the town of Gilroy is home to the annual Gilroy Garlic Festival. As the artichoke is celebrated in Castroville, so is garlic in Gilroy. Although garlic soups can be found in many countries (made with chicken broth and red wine in southern France and with saffron and sherry in Spain, to name a couple), the following is a simple California recipe that I have enjoyed for years. This makes a great lunch, served with a crusty loaf of bread, a good red wine, and a salad.

Place a large sauté pan over medium-high heat and add the oil. Add the onion and sauté for about 5 minutes, until translucent. Add the garlic and sauté for 5 minutes, until the onion is softened and the garlic cloves are slightly browned.

Transfer the onion and garlic to the slow cooker and add the potatoes. Cover with the stock. Cover and cook on low for 6 to 8 hours, until the potatoes are very tender. Using a handheld blender, purée the soup until smooth. Season with salt to taste.

Ladle the soup into individual bowls and garnish with the thyme and sage. Serve at once.

SUGGESTED BEVERAGE: Try the unique Grand Noir from Storrs Winery in Santa Cruz, which is just west of Gilroy, or Bonny Doon's Cigare Volant.

1 tablespoon olive oil

1 yellow onion, coarsely chopped

24 large cloves garlic

2 large russet potatoes, peeled and cut into chunks

6 cups chicken stock (page 91) or water

Salt

Several sprigs of thyme, for garnish

Several sage leaves, sliced, for garnish

GREEN POSOLE

—∘ Serves 4 ∘—

Posole is both an ingredient and a dish. The ingredient is dried field corn soaked in lye or wood ashes in order to loosen the thick skin and make it easier to remove the kernel. It is the primary ingredient in the dish posole, which is a Mexican and southwestern favorite for Christmas Eve and New Year's Day. Posole can be made with either red or green chiles. Canned kernels, known as hominy, can be used, but dried posole stands up the best in the slow cooker. Serve with warm, fresh corn tortillas.

Preheat the broiler. Place the chiles on a baking sheet skin side up. Place under the broiler and broil for 10 minutes, until the skins are blackened. Cover the chiles with a damp kitchen towel and let rest for about 20 minutes. Peel off the skins or scrape them off using a paring knife. Remove the stems and seeds. Chop the chiles.

Combine the posole and water in the slow cooker. Cover and cook on low for about 6 hours, until the posole kernels are plump and softened. Add the roasted chiles, onion, oregano, cumin seeds, and mushrooms and continue cooking on low for 1 to 2 hours. Season to taste with salt.

Spoon into bowls and serve hot, garnished with the feta, green onions, and cilantro. Serve the lime wedges on the side.

SUGGESTED BEVERAGE: A crisp white wine.

6 Anaheim chiles, sliced in half lengthwise

6 ounces dried posole or 1 (12-ounce) can hominy

6 cups chicken stock (page 91) or water

1 large onion, coarsely chopped

2 teaspoons dried Mexican oregano

2 teaspoons cumin seeds, crushed

1 cup sliced cremini mushrooms

Salt

Crumbled feta cheese or *queso fresco*, for garnish

1/4 cup sliced green onion tops, for garnish

1/4 cup coarsely chopped cilantro, for garnish

1 lime, sliced into wedges, for garnish

THREE SISTERS STEW

—∘ Serves 4 ∘—

Because they were generally planted and harvested together and subsequently combined in meals, beans, corn, and squash are known fondly as the three sisters of agriculture to Native Americans of the southwestern United States. Together here they make a healthy, hearty stew.

Combine the beans, water, and tomato sauce in the slow cooker.

Place a large sauté pan over medium-high heat and add the oil. Add the onion and sauté for about 10 minutes, until lightly browned. Transfer to the slow cooker and add the adobo chile and sauce, poblano chile, and garlic. Cover and cook on low for 6 to 8 hours, until the beans are very tender.

Place a sauté pan over medium-high heat and add the chorizo. Cook for 10 to 15 minutes, until browned. Transfer to paper towels to drain.

Add the chorizo, cumin, coriander, chili powder, corn, zucchini, and beer to the cooker and continue cooking for 1 hour, until the zucchini is tender and the corn is cooked. Season to taste with salt.

Serve hot, garnished with the cilantro and sour cream.

SUGGESTED BEVERAGE: "Fire and ice" is often used to refer to the pairing of spicy foods with a cooling, white wine. This concept might work well here. Try a cold, un-oaked Chardonnay or Chenin Blanc.

2 cups dried pinto, anasazi, or red beans, thoroughly rinsed

6 cups chicken stock (page 91) or water

1 cup tomato or marinara sauce

1 tablespoon olive or corn oil

1 yellow onion, coarsely chopped

1 tablespoon canned chile in adobo sauce, with sauce

1 poblano chile, stemmed, seeded, and coarsely chopped

2 cloves garlic, chopped

1/2 pound chorizo sausage, sliced in rounds

1 tablespoon cumin seeds, crushed

1 tablespoon coriander seeds, crushed

1 tablespoon chili powder

3 ears corn, cut into 2-inch lengths

2 zucchini squash, cut in rounds

1/2 cup beer

Salt

1/2 cup coarsely chopped cilantro, for garnish

1/2 cup sour cream, for garnish

BRUNSWICK STEW

—⁀ Serves 4 ⁀—

Virginia historians claim that the original Brunswick Stew was created in Brunswick County, Virginia, in 1828 by a camp cook for a member of the Virginia State Legislature. The original recipe called for squirrel rather than chicken, but most Yankees nowadays pass on the squirrel.

Combine the flour, salt, paprika, and thyme in a large resealable plastic bag. Add the chicken pieces and shake until evenly coated.

Place a large sauté pan over medium-high heat and add the oil. Add the chicken and cook, turning, for 10 to 15 minutes, until browned on all sides. Place the chicken and the pork chops in the slow cooker.

Add the onion to the pan over medium-high heat and sauté in the oil and meat drippings for 10 to 15 minutes, until browned. Place the onion on top of the meat in the cooker.

Mix the Tabasco and Worcestershire sauce into the tomatoes and pour over the chicken. Add the water. Cover and cook on low for about 6 hours, until the chicken is tender. Add the bell pepper, lima beans, and corn and continue cooking for another 1 to 2 hours, until the vegetables are tender. Season with salt to taste.

Remove the chicken and pork from the cooker. Tear the meat off the bones, discard the bones, and return the meat to the stew. Stir in the parsley just before serving.

SUGGESTED BEVERAGE: This is a versatile dish in terms of wine choices. I'd probably prefer a lighter red wine like a Pinot Noir or Sangiovese, or even a good microbrew.

1/2 cup all-purpose flour

1 teaspoon salt

1/2 teaspoon paprika

1/2 teaspoon dried thyme

1 chicken, skinned and cut into pieces

2 tablespoons vegetable oil or unsalted butter

2 smoked or regular pork chops

1 yellow onion, thinly sliced

1/2 teaspoon Tabasco sauce

1 tablespoon Worcestershire sauce

2 cups canned diced tomatoes

1 cup chicken stock (page 91) or water

1 green bell pepper, stemmed, seeded, deveined, and diced

1 (10-ounce) package frozen lima beans, thawed

2 cups fresh or thawed frozen corn kernels

2 tablespoons chopped fresh parsley

Chicken and Seafood Gumbo

—⌐ Serves 4 ⌐—

Like much of the world's good cooking, Creole and Cajun dishes are often whipped up on the spur of the moment using what's on hand. Gumbo's hallmark seasoning is filé powder (pronounced "fee-LAY"), made from dried, ground sassafras leaves, which provide both flavoring and thickening. Filé powder is traditionally added at the very end of the cooking time so it does not lose its flavor or aroma.

Place a large sauté pan over medium-high heat and add the oil. Add the chicken and cook, turning, for 10 to 15 minutes, until browned. Transfer the chicken to a plate. Add the onion and celery to the pan and sauté in the chicken drippings for about 10 minutes, until they are just beginning to color.

Spread the rice evenly in the bottom of the slow cooker and add the chicken, onion, and celery. Add the tomatoes, bell pepper, okra, stock, and bay leaf. Cover and cook on low for 6 to 7 hours, until the meat is very tender. Season to taste with salt.

Place a sauté pan over medium-high heat. Add the bacon and cook, turning, until crispy. Transfer to paper towels to drain, and chop coarsely.

Add the bacon, shrimp, scallops, crab, and thyme to the slow cooker and continue to cook for about 15 minutes. Turn off the heat and stir in the filé powder. Cover and let the gumbo sit for another 15 minutes, just until the shrimp turns pink and the scallops are opaque.

Ladle the gumbo into bowls and serve hot, garnished with the parsley.

SUGGESTED BEVERAGE: Zinfandel seems like the right pairing for gumbo.

2 tablespoons olive oil or unsalted butter

6 chicken legs, skinned

1 large onion, finely chopped

2 large celery stalks, chopped

$1/2$ cup uncooked aromatic brown rice

1 (14-ounce) can chopped tomatoes, undrained

1 green bell pepper, stemmed, seeded, deveined, and diced

1 cup frozen sliced okra

4 cups chicken stock (page 91) or water

1 bay leaf

Salt

2 bacon slices

$1/3$ pound shrimp, raw, unpeeled

$1/3$ pound scallops, raw

$1/3$ pound cooked crabmeat

$1/4$ teaspoon dried thyme

1 to 2 teaspoons filé powder

2 tablespoons chopped fresh parsley, for garnish

Peanut Soup

—⚬ Serves 4 ⚬—

Peanuts reached the American South through a rather circuitous route: Although they were first brought to the United States from Africa in the 1700s, they appear to have originated in South America. The Incas used peanuts in trade, and jars filled with them have been found in ancient Inca graves. This recipe, which may have first come from George Washington Carver's pot, makes an unusual but surprisingly tasty soup.

Combine the peanut butter and 2 cups of the water in a blender and process until smooth.

Place a large sauté pan over medium-high heat and add the butter. Add the onion and sauté for about 5 minutes, until softened. Add the carrot and celery, cover the pan, and sweat for about 10 minutes, until softened.

Transfer the contents of the pan to the slow cooker and add the rice. Add the peanut butter mixture and the remaining 4 cups water. Cover and cook on low for 5 to 7 hours, until the rice is tender. Add the pepper flakes, bell pepper, and peanuts and cook for 1 hour, until the flavors have deepened according to taste. Season to taste with salt.

Ladle into bowls and serve hot, garnished with the chives.

SUGGESTED BEVERAGE: A beer or a dry white wine.

1 cup peanut butter

6 cups chicken stock (page 91) or water

2 tablespoons unsalted butter or peanut or vegetable oil

1 yellow onion, chopped

$1/2$ cup diced carrot

$1/2$ cup diced celery

$1/4$ cup uncooked rice

$1/2$ teaspoon red pepper flakes

$1/2$ green bell pepper, diced

1 cup coarsely ground peanuts

Salt

$1/4$ cup chopped fresh chives or green onions, white and light green parts only, for garnish

White Bean Chili

⁓ Serves 4 ⁓

White chili is usually made with white beans and fresh green chiles rather than the usual red or pink beans and dried red chiles. The bit of cream gives it a very rich mouthfeel. White chili is a wonderful change of pace on a cold winter evening by the fire.

Combine the beans, water, and wine in the slow cooker.

Place a large sauté pan over medium-high heat and add the oil. Add the onion and sauté for about 10 minutes, until lightly browned. Add the garlic and sauté for 5 minutes more.

In a coffee mill or using a mortar and pestle, crush the cumin and coriander seeds and add them to the pan. Stir well.

Transfer the contents of the pan to the slow cooker and add the chiles. Cover and cook on low for 6 to 8 hours, until the beans are tender. About 30 minutes before serving, stir in the oregano, half-and-half, and basil and season to taste with salt.

Ladle into bowls and serve at once, garnished with the cilantro.

SUGGESTED BEVERAGE: A good southwestern or Mexican beer, or a hearty red wine from Arizona or New Mexico.

2 cups dried white beans, thoroughly rinsed

6 cups chicken stock (page 91) or water

1 cup dry white wine

1 tablespoon olive oil or cold-pressed corn oil

1 large white onion, chopped

4 to 6 cloves garlic, finely chopped

2 teaspoons cumin seeds

2 teaspoons coriander seeds

1 (4-ounce) can diced roasted green chiles

1 teaspoon dried Mexican oregano

$1/2$ cup half-and-half or heavy whipping cream

3 fresh basil leaves, coarsely chopped

Salt

$1/2$ cup coarsely chopped cilantro, for garnish

REDEYE STEW

~ Serves 4 ~

Ham with redeye gravy is a southern classic. A cuppa coffee is used to deglaze the pan, and the resulting slurry is poured over the ham slices. I'd bet my buttons that somebody has thrown coffee into the stew for added flavor!

Combine the flour and salt in a large resealable plastic bag. Add the meat in batches and shake until evenly coated.

Place a large sauté pan over medium-high heat and add the oil. Working in batches, add the meat and cook, turning, for 15 minutes, until brown on all sides. Place the meat in the slow cooker and add the potatoes, carrots, onion, garlic, bay leaf, and thyme.

Remove the sauté pan from the heat and pour the coffee into the pan. Using a wooden spoon, scrape any browned bits off the bottom of the pan. Pour the coffee into the cooker and add the water. Cover and cook on low for $5^{1}/_{2}$ to $7^{1}/_{2}$ hours, until the meat is very tender. Add the peas and cook for about 30 minutes.

Ladle into bowls and serve hot.

SUGGESTED BEVERAGE: A flavorful, full-bodied beer or a glass of hearty red wine.

$1^{1}/_{2}$ cups all-purpose flour

2 teaspoons salt

2 tablespoons vegetable oil

$2^{1}/_{2}$ pounds beef stew meat, trimmed of fat

6 small or 2 large russet potatoes, peeled and cut into chunks

2 carrots, cut into large pieces

1 yellow onion, cut into 8 slices

2 cloves garlic, minced

1 bay leaf

2 sprigs thyme

1 cup strong brewed coffee

2 cups water, beer, or wine of any kind

1 cup frozen peas

SALMON, MUSHROOM, SORREL, and AROMATIC RICE BISQUE

—❧ Serves 4 ❧—

Several species of salmon can be found on the Pacific Northwest coast, and morel mushrooms and lemony sorrel are plentiful in the inland woods. They make a nice combination with a good wild rice blend. Serve the soup with crusty bread.

In a small bowl, cover the morels with hot tap water and let stand until soft, about 15 minutes. Drain, reserving the liquid, and coarsely chop. Place a large sauté pan over medium-high heat and add the oil. Add all the fresh mushrooms and the leek and sauté for 10 minutes, until just beginning to color.

Transfer all of the mushrooms, the reserved soaking liquid, and leek to the slow cooker and add the rice and water. Cover and cook on low for about 4 hours, until the rice is tender and the water has been absorbed. Add the salmon, sorrel, cream, and dill. Sprinkle in the flour and stir well. Continue to cook for about 30 minutes, until the salmon is just opaque.

Break the salmon into pieces and stir it into the soup. Season to taste with salt and pepper. Ladle into soup bowls and serve at once.

SUGGESTED BEVERAGE: A luscious Oregon Pinot Noir.

1/2 ounce dried morel mushrooms

2 tablespoons vegetable oil

4 ounces cremini mushrooms, sliced

4 ounces button mushrooms, stemmed, sliced

1 leek, white and light green parts only, thoroughly rinsed, thinly sliced

1/2 cup wild rice blend

4 cups water

1/3 pound boneless skinless salmon steak or fillet

1 cup fresh sorrel or baby spinach leaves, cut into chiffonade

2 cups heavy whipping cream or half-and-half

1 tablespoon chopped fresh dill

About 2 tablespoons quick-mixing flour (such as Wondra)

Salt and freshly ground black pepper

TILLAMOOK CHEDDAR and BEER SOUP

~ Serves 4 ~

Tillamook cheddar cheese is made by a farmer-owned cooperative in Tillamook County, Oregon, that was founded in 1909 by dairy farmers to establish quality control over their product. Today the Tillamook co-op ownership is 150 families strong. And the Portland-based Oregon Brewers Guild, which boasts that Oregon is home to more microbreweries per person than just about anyplace on earth, currently has forty-one small, independent brewing members scattered throughout the state. I can think of fewer toothsome marriages than that of a good, sharp cheddar and a full-flavored beer.

Place a large sauté pan over medium-high heat and add the butter. Add the onion and sauté for about 10 minutes, until lightly browned.

Transfer the onion to the slow cooker and add the celery, potato, stock, and beer. Cover and cook on low for 6 to 8 hours, until the vegetables are tender. Add the Tabasco, mustard, and Worcestershire sauce and stir well.

Using a potato masher, coarsely mash the potatoes until the soup is somewhat thickened but still lumpy. Add the cheese and stir until melted.

Ladle the soup into bowls and serve hot, garnished with the chives and a dollop of crème fraîche if desired.

SUGGESTED BEVERAGE: A delicious Oregon microbrew, or something from your own local brewpub.

1 tablespoon unsalted butter

1 yellow onion, thinly sliced

2 celery stalks with leaves, thinly sliced

1 large russet potato, peeled, cut into 1-inch cubes

6 cups chicken stock (page 91)

1 cup full-bodied beer

$1/4$ teaspoon Tabasco sauce

$1/2$ teaspoon dry mustard

$1/2$ teaspoon Worcestershire sauce

$1/2$ pound sharp cheddar cheese, grated

$1/4$ cup chopped fresh chives, for garnish

$1/4$ cup crème fraîche or sour cream, for garnish (optional)

Walla Walla Onion Soup

—✧ Serves 4 ✧—

Although Walla Walla, Washington, is home to more than sixty wineries, it is also famous for the Walla Walla onion—a big sweetie similar to a Vidalia or a Maui onion. Legend has it that a French soldier found the seeds of a large, sweet onion on the island of Corsica and brought it to Walla Walla. The onion owes its yummy flavor to a high water and low sulfur content, and makes the sweetest of onion soups. For an extra treat, top the soup with a crouton of French bread covered with melted Gruyère cheese.

Combine the onions and butter in the slow cooker. Cover and cook on high for 1 hour, then decrease the heat to low. Cover and cook, stirring occasionally, for about 4 hours, until the onions are evenly browned. Sprinkle in the flour and stir well. Add the wine and stock and cook on low for 2 hours, allowing the flavors to meld. Stir in the port and season to taste with salt and pepper.

Ladle into bowls, sprinkle with the parsley, and serve at once.

SUGGESTED BEVERAGE: A Washington state microbrew or a medium- to full-bodied red wine from the Walla Walla Valley.

4 pounds Walla Walla or any large, sweet onions, thinly sliced

3 tablespoons unsalted butter

3 tablespoons quick-mixing flour (such as Wondra)

1 cup dry red or white wine

5 cups beef stock (page 91) or water

2 tablespoons port

Salt and freshly ground black pepper

Chopped fresh parsley, for garnish

SAN FRANCISCO CIOPPINO

—◦ Serves 4 ◦—

The word cioppino *means "fish stew" in the Ligurian dialect. Like all classic fishermen stews, the recipe isn't written in stone. Traditionally, the contents of the dish depend on the catch of the day. At Fisherman's Wharf in San Francisco, you can count on crab being the main attraction; crab cioppino has been a favorite in the Bay Area for many years. The soup can cook all day if you so desire, but for best results the seafood should really be tossed in at the last minute. Serve it with crusty sourdough bread to sop up the juices.*

Place a large sauté pan over medium-high heat and add the oil. Add the onion and sauté for about 5 minutes, until softened. Add the garlic and sauté for 2 minutes.

Transfer the contents of the pan to the slow cooker and add the tomatoes, stock, Tabasco sauce, wine, basil, and bay leaf. Cover and cook on low for 4 to 6 hours (though it could be left on for 8 hours if necessary), until the stock is rich and hot, ready for the fish.

About 30 minutes before serving, add the shrimp, crab, clams, and fish. Cover and cook on high for about 30 minutes, until the fish turns opaque. Season to taste with salt and pepper and serve garnished with a sprinkling of the parsley.

SUGGESTED BEVERAGE: A full-bodied red wine; Zinfandel or Syrah would do nicely.

$1/4$ cup olive oil

1 yellow onion, finely chopped

4 cloves garlic, finely chopped

2 (16-ounce) cans chopped tomatoes, undrained

2 cups fish or chicken stock (page 91), or water

Dash of Tabasco sauce

1 cup hearty red wine

3 tablespoons fresh basil, cut into chiffonade

1 bay leaf

$1/2$ pound shrimp, raw, unpeeled

1 small cooked crab, cut into serving pieces

6 or 8 small clams

$1/2$ pound red snapper, halibut, or other white fish

Salt and freshly ground black pepper

$1/4$ cup chopped fresh parsley, for garnish

Butternut Squash and Apple Soup

—◦ Serves 4 ◦—

Apples were one of the first tree crops to be planted in America and were originally used to make hard cider. The flavor of this soup is predominantly of squash with just a hint of apple for extra sweetness and a touch of acidity.

Place a large sauté pan over medium-high heat and add the butter. Add the onion and celery and sauté for about 5 minutes, until softened.

Place the squash and apple in the slow cooker. Add the onion and celery and the stock.

Cover and cook on low for about 6 hours, until the squash and apples are quite tender. Combine the cinnamon, cloves, and allspice in a coffee mill or using a mortar and pestle and grind to a coarse powder. Half an hour before serving, add the spices to the cooker.

Using a handheld blender, carefully purée the soup until smooth. Season to taste with salt and pepper.

Ladle into bowls and serve warm, garnished with the chives and a dollop of sour cream.

SUGGESTED BEVERAGE: An un-oaked Chardonnay or a Gewürztraminer.

2 tablespoons unsalted butter

1 cup chopped yellow onion

$^1/_2$ cup sliced celery stalks and leaves

1 large butternut squash, peeled and cut into cubes

1 small apple, peeled, cored, and cut into chunks

6 cups chicken stock (page 91) or water

2 cinnamon sticks

6 whole cloves

6 allspice berries

Salt and freshly ground black pepper

Chopped fresh chives, for garnish

Sour cream, for garnish.

CLAM and POTATO CHOWDER

—◦ Serves 4 ◦—

The earliest American recipes for chowder called for fish rather than clams or shellfish and were prepared by layering the fish, salt pork, and biscuits (all shipboard staples) in a pot and cooking them for hours over a fire. This recipe calls for canned clams simply because those are the most easily accessible, but you can cook and use fresh clams as well.

Combine 3 tablespoons of butter and the flour in a saucepan over medium-high heat. Cook, stirring constantly, for 5 minutes, until the butter begins to froth and brown lightly. Slowly add the water or stock, stirring constantly to ensure smooth blending, for about 10 to 15 minutes, until the sauce is thick enough to coat the back of a spoon.

Place a large sauté pan over medium-high heat and add the remaining tablespoon of butter. Add the onion, leek, and celery and sauté for about 5 minutes, until just translucent.

Transfer the contents of the pan to the slow cooker and add the potatoes and thyme. Pour in the sauce. Cover and cook on low for about 6 hours, until the potatoes are tender.

Place a sauté pan over medium-high heat. Add the bacon and cook, turning, until crispy. Transfer to paper towels to drain, and then dice.

Stir the half-and-half, bacon, and clams into the chowder and continue to cook for 30 minutes, until heated through.

Ladle into bowls and serve garnished with the parsley.

VARIATIONS: To make a good vegetarian chowder, omit the clams and bacon and add 3 cups of fresh or frozen corn or mixed vegetables.

SUGGESTED BEVERAGE: Hard cider, beer, or ale would be the best, but a crisp Gewürztraminer, Pinot Grigio, Sauvignon Blanc, or other light-to-medium white wine would also go well.

4 tablespoons unsalted butter

3 tablespoons all-purpose flour

3 cups clam juice, fish or chicken stock (page 91), or water

1 small yellow onion, diced

1 leek, white and light green parts only, thoroughly washer, thinly sliced

2 small inner celery stalks, sliced

2 large russet potatoes, peeled and cut into $1/2$-inch pieces, or 1 pound red potatoes, cut into $1/2$-inch pieces

1 sprig thyme

3 thick-cut bacon slices or pancetta slices

3 cups half-and-half or milk

3 ($6^1/2$-ounce) cans clams, coarsely chopped

Chopped fresh parsley, for garnish

IOWA CORN CHOWDER

—☙ Serves 4 ☙—

Iowa is the country's largest producer of corn, with more than 12,000 acres planted to the crop and nearly 2 million bushels harvested annually. Sadly, much of it is now genetically modified, so if you want to avoid genetically modified foods, buy organic.

Place a large sauté pan over medium-high heat and add the butter. Add the onion and sauté for about 10 minutes, until lightly browned. Transfer to the slow cooker and add 2 cups of the corn and the water. Cover and cook on low for 5 to 6 hours, until the chowder is rich and sweet.

Using a handheld blender, carefully purée the soup until smooth. Add the cream and remaining 1 cup corn and stir well. Cover and cook for about 20 minutes, until heated through. Season to taste with salt and pepper.

Ladle into bowls and serve hot, garnished with the chives.

SUGGESTED BEVERAGE: A Pinot Blanc, Pinot Gris, or Sauvignon Blanc from one of Iowa's forty-four licensed wineries.

1 tablespoon unsalted butter

1 yellow onion, coarsely chopped

3 cups fresh or frozen corn kernels

4 cups vegetable stock, chicken stock (page 91), or water

2 cups heavy whipping cream or half-and-half

Salt and freshly ground black pepper

Chopped fresh chives, for garnish

ROASTED CARROT-PARSNIP SOUP

—◌ Serves 4 ◌—

Hearty winter root vegetables take well to long hours in the slow cooker. Turnips or rutabagas can be substituted for the parsnips in this easy slow-cooker classic. For a richer flavor, treat yourself to a bit of cream.

Put the butter or oil in the slow cooker. Add the carrots, parsnips, onion, and garlic and cook on low for about 1 hour, or until the vegetables begin to brown. (The slight caramelization of the vegetables adds an extra flavor dimension to this soup, but you can leave this step out if you're pressed for time: omit the butter or oil and add the vegetables and water to the slow cooker all at once.)

Pour in the water and cook on low for 4 hours, until the vegetables are very tender.

Using a handheld blender, purée the vegetables in the slow cooker.

Season with salt and add the cream, if using.

Serve at once, garnished with chervil, parsley, or chives, or a combination of all three.

SUGGESTED BEVERAGE: A hearty red, such as a Zinfandel or Syrah, or a rosé.

1 pound carrots, peeled and cut into chunks

2 small parsnips, peeled and cut into chunks

1/2 yellow onion, coarsely chopped

3 cloves garlic

5 cups chicken stock (page 91) or water

Salt

1/2 cup cream or whole milk (optional)

Chopped fresh chervil, parsley, or chives, for garnish

Meat & Fish

BASQUE LAMB SHANKS

—⚬ Serves 4 ⚬—

Spanish Basque immigrants first arrived in the United States in the mid-1800s. This recipe contains typical ingredients found in a Basque lamb stew, which is often served at traditional family-style restaurants in the Basque communities that can still be found throughout the Pacific Northwest and West. I suggest you cook it until the meat is just about to fall off the bone.

Combine the flour and salt in a resealable plastic bag. One at a time, add the lamb shanks and shake until evenly coated.

Place a large sauté pan over medium-high heat and add the oil. Add the lamb and cook, turning, for 15 to 20 minutes, until browned on all sides.

Transfer the lamb to the slow cooker. Add the beans, garlic, water, wine, and tomatoes. Cover and cook on low for about 5 hours. Add the squash and cook on low for another 3 hours, until the lamb and squash are very tender. (In a pinch, the squash can be added at the beginning of cooking and left in the entire time.)

Just before serving, stir in the olives and thyme and season to taste with salt and pepper.

SUGGESTED BEVERAGE: Any gutsy, hearty red wine such as a Zinfandel, Syrah, a Spanish import, or even, if one can be found on rare occasion, a Basque wine.

1 cup all-purpose flour

1 teaspoon salt

4 small lamb shanks

3 tablespoons olive oil

1 cup dried white beans

6 cloves garlic

1 cup chicken or beef stock (page 91), or water

1 cup red wine

1 (14-ounce) can diced tomatoes, undrained

$^1/_2$ butternut squash, peeled and cut into $1^1/_2$-inch cubes

$^1/_2$ cup pitted black olives

2 sprigs thyme

Freshly ground black pepper

PORK ROAST with APPLES, CIDER, and CREAM

—ॐ Serves 4 ॐ—

At certain times of the year, parts of Northern California's Sonoma County sprout masses of wild mushrooms, and at one time apple orchards covered many of the hills now blanketed with vineyards. Gone today are many of those venerable old trees, but remnants of some orchards remain, as does the heritage that inspired this savory slow-cooked meal.

Place a large sauté pan over medium-high heat and add the oil. Add the pork and cook, turning, for about 15 minutes, until evenly browned on all sides. Transfer the meat to the slow cooker.

Add the onion to the pan and sauté in the oil for about 7 minutes, until it just begins to brown. Add the mushrooms and sauté for 5 minutes, until tender. Add the apple juice and wine and cook for 10 minutes, until reduced in half, scraping any bits from the bottom of the pan.

Pour the sauce and vegetables over the roast. Cover and cook on low for about 6 hours, until the meat is very tender and has reached an internal temperature of at least 165°F. Remove the roast from the slow cooker and set aside on a plate. Add the cream and apple to the juices in the slow cooker and stir well. Return the meat to the slow cooker and continue cooking on high for 30 minutes.

Preheat the oven to 350°F. Spread the walnuts on a baking sheet and toast, stirring occasionally, for 7 to 10 minutes, until evenly browned. Remove from the oven and allow to cool. When cool enough to handle, coarsely chop the walnuts.

Remove the pork from the slow cooker and cut into serving slices. Arrange the pork on plates and spoon on the sauce and apples. Garnish each serving with the walnuts and serve at once.

SUGGESTED BEVERAGE: A Russian River Valley Chardonnay.

2 tablespoons vegetable or grape seed oil

2¹/₂-pound pork loin roast, trimmed of fat

1 yellow onion, chopped

1 ounce assorted fresh wild mushrooms, stemmed, thoroughly cleaned

1 cup apple juice or apple cider

¹/₂ cup Chardonnay or other white wine

1 cup heavy whipping cream

1 pippin or other tart, firm-fleshed apple, sliced

1 cup walnuts

KOREAN-STYLE RIBS

—⌾ Serves 4 ⌾—

I first ate Korean ribs years ago in San Francisco's Bay Area, where there are many fine Korean restaurants. Although Korean ribs are usually barbecued, this slow-cooked version is a good approximation of the real deal, and the result is mouthwatering.

Place a large sauté pan over medium-high heat. Add the ribs and cook, turning, for 15 to 20 minutes, until browned on all sides. Transfer the ribs to the slow cooker.

In a bowl, combine the soy sauce, orange juice, vinegar, ginger, garlic, sesame oil, and brown sugar and mix well. Pour the sauce over the ribs. Cover and cook on low for 6 to 8 hours, until the meat is very tender.

To serve, arrange the ribs on plates or a serving platter and spoon the sauce on top. Garnish with the sesame seeds and green onions and serve at once.

SUGGESTED BEVERAGE: A Korean or Japanese beer.

3 pounds pork or beef ribs, trimmed of excess fat

1/2 cup soy sauce

1 cup freshly squeezed orange or tangerine juice

2 tablespoons rice vinegar

1 tablespoon finely minced or grated fresh peeled ginger

3 cloves garlic, finely minced

2 tablespoons toasted sesame oil

2 tablespoons brown sugar or honey

3 tablespoons toasted sesame seeds, for garnish

2 green onions, green parts only, thinly sliced, for garnish

PULLED PORK with BARBECUE SAUCE

— Serves 4 —

Pulled pork with barbecue sauce is a southern classic—true comfort food. It's delicious in Sloppy Joe sandwiches or all by itself over rice. This recipe couldn't be easier to make: just let it cook until the meat falls apart. For a lighter version, use half a turkey breast instead of pork.

Place the pork in the slow cooker.

In a bowl, combine the ketchup, vinegar, water, onion, garlic, chili powder, and Worcestershire sauce and stir well. Pour the sauce over the roast. Cover and cook on low for 8 to 10 hours, until the meat falls apart.

Remove the pork from the cooker and allow to cool slightly. Remove and discard any bones. Pull the meat into shreds using your fingers or two forks. Return the meat to the cooker and stir into the sauce. Serve warm.

SUGGESTED BEVERAGE: A pilsner or light-colored beer.

2 pounds pork roast (any cut)

2 cups ketchup

3 tablespoons apple cider vinegar

1 cup water

1 small yellow onion, finely chopped

5 cloves garlic, minced

1 tablespoon chili powder

1 tablespoon Worcestershire sauce

Italian American Pork Chops

~ Serves 4 ~

This recipe comes from my friend Nick Palumbo, owner of Palumbo Family Vineyards and Winery in Temecula, California. The great red sauce and thick, tender pork is even more scrumptious over a serving of buttery mashed potatoes.

To prepare the sauce, place a large sauté pan over medium-high heat and add the oil. Add the onion, carrots, garlic, and celery and sauté for about 5 minutes, until soft but not browned.

Transfer the vegetables to the slow cooker and add the tomatoes, tomato paste, oregano, and fennel and season with salt and pepper. Cover and cook on low for about 8 hours. Transfer the sauce to a covered container.

To prepare the chops, combine the flour and salt in a resealable plastic bag. Place the eggs in a shallow dish. Dip each chop into the eggs to coat thoroughly. One at a time, place the chops in the bag and shake until evenly coated.

Place a large sauté pan over medium-high heat and add the oil. Add the pork chops and cook, turning, for about 15 minutes, until browned on both sides.

Place the chops in the slow cooker and pour 4 cups of the sauce over the top. Cover and cook on low for 6 to 8 hours, until the meat is very tender.

Place a chop on each plate and generously spoon the sauce over the top. Serve at once.

SUGGESTED BEVERAGE: Palumbo Family Vineyards Sangiovese.

Marinara Sauce
Makes 4 to 5 cups

1 tablespoon olive oil

1 large onion, finely chopped

2 large carrots, finely chopped

4 cloves garlic, finely chopped

4 celery stalks, finely chopped

1 (35-ounce) can diced tomatoes

1 (4-ounce) can tomato paste

2 teaspoons dried oregano

1/2 teaspoon fennel seeds

Salt and freshly ground black pepper

Pork Chops

1 cup all-purpose flour

2 teaspoons salt

3 eggs, lightly beaten

4 thick center-cut pork chops, trimmed of fat

3 tablespoons olive oil

BRATWURST, RED CABBAGE, and APPLES

—∘ Serves 4 ∘—

This dish pays homage to the many German immigrants that have made their homes in the Midwest and the northern states over the last two hundred years. While fine German bratwurst is to die for, any high-quality sausage will taste wonderful in this hearty dish.

Place a sauté pan over medium-high heat. Add the bratwurst and cook, turning, for about 15 minutes, until well browned.

In a small bowl, combine the vinegar, sugar, and beer and mix until the sugar dissolves.

In a large bowl, combine the cabbage, onions, caraway seeds, and apples and toss well with your hands. Season with salt and pepper. Transfer to the slow cooker and pour in the vinegar mixture. Place the bratwurst on top. Cover and cook on low for 4 to 6 hours, until the cabbage is tender to your taste.

Divide the bratwurst and vegetables evenly among plates and serve hot.

SUGGESTED BEVERAGE: No fancy wine. Hard cider or beer's the ticket.

1^1/2 pounds bratwurst

^{1}/4 cup apple cider vinegar

1 tablespoon sugar

1 cup beer

1 head red cabbage, quartered, cored, and sliced

2 yellow onions, thinly sliced

1 teaspoon caraway seeds

2 pippin or small Granny Smith apples, cored, quartered and thinly sliced

Salt and freshly ground black pepper

OLD-FASHIONED POT ROAST

—⚬ Serves 4 ⚬—

Sensible and practical—the quintessential qualities of a colonial American dish. Pot roasts hold up extraordinarily well to a long cooking period—perfect for preparing during long days of hard work.

Combine the all-purpose flour and salt in a large resealable plastic bag. Add the meat and shake until evenly coated.

Place a large sauté pan over medium-high heat and add the oil. Add the meat and cook, turning, for about 15 minutes, until browned on all sides. Transfer the meat to the slow cooker.

In a small bowl, combine the water and quick-mixing flour and stir to form a slurry.

Arrange the potatoes, carrots, and onions on top of the meat and pour in the slurry and the vinegar. Cover and cook on low for about 8 hours, until the meat is very tender.

Evenly divide the meat and vegetables among dinner plates and spoon on the thickened juices. Serve at once.

SUGGESTED BEVERAGE: A good hearty beer, a hard cider from one of New England's microbreweries, or a hearty red wine such as a full-bodied Merlot.

1 cup all-purpose flour

1 teaspoon salt

1 ($2^1/2$- to 3-pound) piece beef chuck, trimmed of fat

2 tablespoons vegetable oil

1 cup beef stock (page 91) or water

2 tablespoons quick-mixing flour (such as Wondra)

6 red potatoes, unpeeled, halved

6 small carrots

2 yellow onions, quartered

$1/3$ cup apple cider vinegar

Freshly ground black pepper

MEATLOAF

—◌ Serves 4 ◌—

Every family in America probably has a favorite recipe for meatloaf. It's one of those dishes that make us think of home. Always spice a meatloaf generously, as the spices dissipate during cooking. Add plenty of moist ingredients such as tomato sauce or ketchup, eggs, and if need be, stock.

Line the slow cooker with two sheets of aluminum foil for easy removal of the meatloaf.

In a large bowl, combine the beef, onions, celery, bell pepper, garlic, eggs, and bread and season with salt and pepper. Mix well with your hands and shape into an oblong loaf (or if you are using a round slow cooker, into a round loaf).

Place the loaf into the slow cooker and pour the ketchup evenly over the top. Cover and cook on low for 6 to 7 hours, until an instant-read thermometer inserted into the center of the loaf registers 165°F and the meat is browned.

Lift the meatloaf from the cooker by gently grasping the aluminum foil and pulling it out. Let it rest for about 20 minutes before slicing and serving.

SUGGESTED BEVERAGE: A good Syrah or medium-to full-bodied red wine.

2 pounds lean ground beef, pork, veal, or turkey

2 yellow onions, chopped

2 celery stalks, chopped

1 green bell pepper, stemmed, seeded, deveined, and chopped

2 cloves garlic, finely chopped

2 eggs

1 cup finely diced bread

Salt and freshly ground black pepper

1 cup ketchup

CHICKEN ADOBO

—⚬ Serves 4 ⚬—

The national dish of the Philippines, chicken adobo is popular in Filipino immigrant communities all over the world, including the Hawaiian Islands. This recipe comes from my auntie's friend, Violet Sadural, who was born in the Philippines and now lives in Honolulu. Beef, fish, vegetables, chicken, and pork can all be cooked adobo style. Although open to the discretion of each cook, the basic adobo ingredients are usually vinegar, soy sauce, garlic, peppercorns, and sometimes ginger. The dish is served simply, with white rice and stir-fried vegetables.

Place the chicken in the slow cooker. Add the garlic, bay leaves, soy sauce, vinegar, ginger, peppercorns, and brown sugar and toss until thoroughly mixed. In a small bowl, combine the cornstarch and stock and mix to form a slurry. Add to the pot and gently stir in.

Cover and cook on low for 6 to 8 hours, until the meat is very tender. Leave the chicken pieces whole or shred the meat, whatever your preference. Serve at once, garnished with the green onions.

SUGGESTED BEVERAGE: For an adventuresome experiment, try a bottle of Volcano Winery's Symphony Dry. The winery is located on the side of an active volcano on the Big Island of Hawaii.

1 (3-pound) frying chicken, skinned and cut into serving pieces

5 cloves garlic, crushed

2 bay leaves

$^3/_4$ cup soy sauce

$^1/_4$ cup apple cider vinegar or distilled white vinegar

1 tablespoon finely grated fresh peeled ginger

$^1/_4$ teaspoon crushed black peppercorns

1 tablespoon brown sugar

1 tablespoon cornstarch

$^1/_4$ cup chicken stock (page 91)

Green onions, white and light green parts, sliced, for garnish

YANKEE CHICKEN POTPIE

—✦ Serves 4 ✦—

This recipe departs from the traditional pastry crust potpie, using instead a layer of herb and garlic mashed potatoes. The topping is so delicious it can just as easily be served alone as a side dish. If you want to be true to your slow cooker and use it for both steps, the potatoes need to be made first and set aside, or, if you're lucky enough to have two slow cookers, at the same time as the filling. They can, however, be made just as easily on a stovetop.

To prepare the crust, place the potatoes in the slow cooker and cover with cold water. Cover and cook on low for about 4 hours, until the potatoes are tender when pierced with a fork. Drain off the water and increase the heat to high. Cook for about 30 minutes, until dry. Add the sour cream, garlic, and salt and pepper to taste. Using a potato masher, mash the potatoes to your desired consistency. Add the chives at the last minute and mix in thoroughly.

If using the conventional stovetop method, cut the potatoes in chunks and boil until very soft, about 30 minutes. Remove the pot from the heat and drain off the water. Add the sour cream, garlic, and salt and pepper to taste. Using a potato masher, mash the potatoes to your desired consistency. Add the chives at the last minute and mix in thoroughly.

To prepare the filling, place a large saucepan over high heat and add 3 tablespoons of the butter. Add the flour and cook, stirring constantly, for about 5 minutes, until lightly browned. Add the stock and continue cooking and stirring for 15 minutes, until the mixture thickens enough to coat the back of a spoon. Add the nutmeg and salt and pepper to taste.

Mashed Potato Crust

4 large russet potatoes
  (optionally peeled)

1 cup sour cream or half-and-half

4 cloves garlic, pressed

Salt and freshly ground black
  pepper

1/4 cup finely chopped fresh
  chives

Filling

4 tablespoons unsalted butter

1/4 cup all-purpose flour

2 cups chicken stock (page 91)
  or milk

Pinch of freshly ground nutmeg

Salt and freshly ground black
  pepper

1 leek, white and light green parts
  only, thoroughly washed, thinly
  sliced

Place a sauté pan over medium-high heat and add the remaining tablespoon of butter. Add the leek, carrots, and celery and sauté for about 10 minutes, just until soft. Transfer to the slow cooker and add the chicken and sauce. Gently fold in the peas and fresh tarragon. Cover and cook on low for about 4 hours, until the vegetables are tender and the chicken is cooked through.

Spoon the potato crust over the top of the filling and cook for about 1 hour, until the potatoes brown at the edges. Garnish with the parsley and serve piping hot.

SUGGESTED BEVERAGE: A crisp, un-oaked Chardonnay, Sauvignon Blanc, or Chenin Blanc, but a Pinot would work too.

3 carrots, peeled and diced or cut into rounds

2 celery stalks, sliced

2 cups chicken or turkey breasts, cubed (about 2 cups)

1 cup frozen or fresh peas

1 tablespoon coarsely chopped fresh tarragon

1 tablespoon coarsely chopped fresh parsley

Simple Poached Salmon

—⟡ Serves 4 ⟡—

Poaching salmon, or any fish for that matter, in the slow cooker is a no-brainer. Although it isn't a traditional dish for long, slow cooking, it is one of the things that the low, even temperatures of the slow cooker does well with. Poached salmon, needing no oil to cook, makes a light lunch paired with lemon rice, steamed vegetables, and salad, or a sumptuous dinner with herbed mashed potatoes and grilled vegetables.

Combine the water and wine in the slow cooker and heat on high for 20 to 30 minutes. Add the onion, lemon, dill, salt, and salmon.

Cover and cook on high for about 20 minutes, until the salmon is opaque and cooked through according to taste. Serve hot or cold.

SUGGESTED BEVERAGE: Salmon, a classic Pacific Northwest ingredient, generally fits like a glove with pinot noir, Oregon's most beloved grape.

1 cup water

$1/2$ cup dry white wine

1 yellow onion slice

1 lemon slice

1 sprig dill

$1/2$ teaspoon salt

4 (6-ounce) salmon fillets

COUNTRY HAM in PINEAPPLE SAUCE with DRIED CHERRIES and RAISINS

—⁘ Serves 4 ⁘—

Nothing can compare to a Virginia baked ham, but any good-quality ham used in this recipe will yield surprisingly delicious results. This is truly one of those foolproof throw-everything-in-the-cooker-and-walk-away kind of dishes. Mashed potatoes and green beans make a great accompaniment.

Stud the ham with the cloves, then place in the slow cooker.

Drain the pineapple juice into a bowl and add the cornstarch. Stir until thoroughly blended. Add the pineapple and preserves and mix well. Pour and spoon over the ham.

Cover and cook on low for 5 to 7 hours. Sprinkle on the cherries and raisins and continue to cook for 1 hour, until the meat is very tender.

Remove the ham from the sauce and allow to cool for about 15 minutes on a cutting board. Cut into slices and arrange on plates or a serving platter. Generously spoon the sauce over the meat and serve at once.

SUGGESTED BEVERAGE: A crisp, aromatic white wine such as a Gewürztraminer or a Sauvignon Blanc Musqué with a bit of residual sugar. Or explore some of the well-made wines now coming out of Virginia.

1 (4-pound) bone-in ham

10 whole cloves

1 (20-ounce) can crushed pineapple, undrained

1 tablespoon cornstarch

1 (18-ounce) jar pineapple-apricot preserves

1/4 cup dried sour cherries

1/4 cup golden raisins or currants

TURKEY with CRANBERRIES

—◦ Serves 4 ◦—

Cranberries are native to North America and were used by indigenous peoples long before the Pilgrims arrived. They were mashed with deer meat for pemmican because their natural benzoic acid helps slow spoilage. For a slightly untraditional cranberry sauce, the dried berries, citrus flavor, and port beautifully complement a juicy turkey. Serve with wild rice pilaf or mashed potatoes.

Place a large sauté pan over medium-high heat and add the oil. Add the onions and sauté for about 10 minutes, until lightly browned.

In a small bowl, combine the port and cornstarch and mix to form a slurry. Add to the sauté pan and stir well. Add the stock and cook, stirring, over medium-high heat for about 7 minutes, until the sauce thickens and becomes translucent.

Place the turkey in the slow cooker and pour in the sauce. Add the cranberries, cinnamon, and orange slices. Cover and cook on low for 6 to 8 hours, until the turkey is very tender and cooked through and the sauce is thick. Serve at once.

SUGGESTED BEVERAGE: The crispness and acidity of a Sauvignon Blanc or a lighter Pinot Noir matches the acidity of the cranberries.

1 tablespoon canola or vegetable oil

2 yellow onions, thinly sliced

$2/3$ cup port

1 tablespoon cornstarch

2 cups chicken or turkey stock (page 91), or water

$1/2$ turkey breast, skinned and trimmed of fat

8 ounces dried cranberries (orange flavored makes a nice variation)

1 cinnamon stick

1 orange, tangerine, or blood orange, unpeeled, sliced thinly

BACALHAU

—⚬ Serves 4 ⚬—

Preserved cod holds up well to several hours in the slow cooker. Salting and drying fish and packing it in barrels is a time-honored method of preservation brought to California by Portuguese immigrants like my grandmother's people, who came to this country from their home in the Azores.

Soak the cod in the refrigerator in two or three changes of water overnight. Remove any bones or skin and, using your fingers, shred the flesh.

Place a large sauté pan over medium-high heat and add the oil. Sauté the onion until golden brown, about 15 minutes. Add the garlic and cook for 2 minutes.

Coat the bottom of the slow cooker with olive oil. Arrange half of the sliced potatoes in the bottom of the cooker. Cover with a layer of half the fish, followed by a layer of half the onion mixture. Pour half of the crushed tomatoes on top.

Repeat the layering with the remaining potatoes, fish, onion mixture, and tomatoes.

Cover and cook on low for 4 to 6 hours, until the potatoes are very tender.

A half hour before serving, pour in the cream evenly over the fish.

Divide the fish and vegetables among 4 shallow bowls and garnish each with 5 green olives and a dusting of Parmesan cheese. Serve hot with a loaf of crusty bread.

SUGGESTED BEVERAGE: A crisp Sauvignon Blanc or Gewürztraminer.

1 pound salt cod

1/4 cup olive oil, plus extra for coating

1 large yellow onion, sliced

2 cloves garlic, minced

4 large potatoes, peeled and sliced

1 (28-ounce) can crushed tomatoes

1/2 cup heavy whipping cream

20 stuffed green olives, for garnish

2 tablespoons grated Parmesan cheese, for garnish

Sides

GRITS with JACK CHEESE, CHILES, and GREENS

—ᜀ Serves 4 ᜀ—

Spring greens are an excellent source of vitamins A and C, which makes them all the better to eat after a long winter. Tender arugula or baby spinach enrich the corn, making a perfect accompaniment to chili, grilled steak, or a vegetarian main dish.

Preheat the broiler. Slice the chile in half, discarding its veins and seeds, and arrange skin side up on a baking sheet. Place under the broiler and grill for about 10 minutes, until the skin is blackened. Cover the chile with a damp kitchen towel and let rest for about 20 minutes. Peel off the skin or scrape it off using a paring knife. Chop the chile.

Place the grits, water, salt, and butter in the slow cooker. Cover and cook on low for about 3 hours, until the water is absorbed and the grits are tender. Thirty minutes before serving, stir in the onion, arugula, roasted chile, and cheese. Season to taste with salt and pepper.

Ladle into bowls and top each portion with a sprinkling of cheese. Serve at once.

SUGGESTED BEVERAGE: A light-colored beer.

1 Anaheim chile, or 2 tablespoons canned diced jalapeño chiles

1 cup coarse grits

4 cups chicken stock (page 91) or water

1 teaspoon salt

1 tablespoon unsalted butter

1 yellow onion, chopped

1 cup loosely packed baby arugula or spinach

Salt and freshly ground black pepper

2 ounces Monterey Jack, grated

Sun-Dried Tomato Risotto

—◦ Serves 4 ◦—

This recipe comes from the grandmother of Mike Thompson, the U.S. congressman who represents the California counties of Napa, Sonoma, Lake, Del Norte, Humboldt, and Mendocino—wine country. Home to many Italian immigrants, the region inspires this red wine and sun-dried tomato risotto. The grandmotherly way to prepare it is, of course, to use a ladle rather than a measuring cup to add stock.

Place a large sauté pan over medium-high heat and add the butter and olive oil. Add the onion and sauté for about 7 minutes, until translucent. Add the garlic and rice and sauté for 5 minutes, until the rice is slightly translucent.

Transfer the contents of the pan to the slow cooker and add the wine, stock, and sun-dried tomatoes. Cover and cook on high for about 2 hours, until the rice is tender and the liquid has been absorbed. Just before serving, stir in the cheese and season with salt and pepper to taste.

SUGGESTED BEVERAGE: Since you already have a bottle of red wine open to prepare this unusual risotto, it's a natural pairing. I suggest a Napa Cab.

3 tablespoons unsalted butter

1 tablespoon olive oil

$1/2$ yellow onion, diced

3 cloves garlic, crushed

$1^1/2$ cups Arborio rice

1 cup red wine

5 to 6 cups chicken stock (page 91)

$1/4$ cup sun-dried tomatoes packed in oil, drained and minced

About $1/2$ cup grated Parmigiano-Reggiano cheese

Salt and freshly ground black pepper

Shredded Meat for Tacos, Tortillas, Burritos, and Casseroles

—◦ Makes 3 pounds of shredded meat ◦—

Shredded meat is a staple in both Mexican and southwestern kitchens, and is a perfect side to make in a slow cooker. It can be used to fill tacos, burritos, and tostadas or can just be tossed with scrambled eggs for breakfast. The following simple recipe can be made with beef, pork, or even turkey. Cooking times may vary according to type and cut of meat, but in general, when your desired result is meat that can easily be shredded, anything cooked for 6 to 8 hours ought to work out fine.

Trim the meat of all fat. Place the meat, salt, onion, garlic, and water in the slow cooker. Cover and cook on low for about 8 hours, until the meat is very tender. Remove the meat from the cooker, allow it to cool, and then shred it using your fingers or 2 forks. The stock can be frozen for later use in soups or stews.

SUGGESTED BEVERAGE: A blond beer.

2 pounds beef chuck or brisket, pork butt or shoulder, or turkey breast or leg

1 teaspoon salt

1 yellow onion, cut into large chunks

4 cloves garlic, whole

1 quart water

SOUTHWESTERN CORNBREAD PUDDING

—ᵒ Serves 4 ᵒ—

This bread pudding is savory, not sweet. A melding of the delicious southwestern flavors of corn, chiles, coriander, cumin, and cheese, it makes a wonderful side dish to a roasted loin of pork or beef.

To make the cornbread, preheat the oven to 400°F. Combine all the ingredients in a bowl and mix well. Pour the batter into a greased 9 by 9-inch baking pan and bake for about 25 minutes, until the top is golden brown. Remove the cornbread from the oven and allow to cool slightly.

When cool enough to handle, cut or break the cornbread into 1½-inch cubes and place in a bowl. Using your hands, mix in the corn kernels, chile, green onions, cheddar, Monterey Jack, chard, coriander, and cumin. Transfer to the slow cooker.

In a blender, combine the buttermilk, eggs, and enchilada sauce and mix well. Pour over the ingredients in the cooker. Cover and cook on low for about 3 hours, until the pudding is set. Serve immediately.

SUGGESTED BEVERAGE: A southwestern beer, or even a lighter style, fruity red wine.

Cornbread

1 cup yellow cornmeal

1 cup all-purpose flour

1/3 cup sugar

1 teaspoon baking soda

2 teaspoons baking powder

1 cup buttermilk

2 eggs

4 tablespoons melted unsalted butter or vegetable oil

1½ cups fresh or frozen corn kernels

1 long green Anaheim or poblano chile, stemmed, seeded, and diced

1/2 cup chopped green onions, white and light green parts

1 cup grated sharp cheddar cheese

1 cup grated Monterey Jack cheese

2 cups very coarsely chopped fresh chard leaves and stems or spinach

1 teaspoon coriander seeds, crushed

1 teaspoon cumin seeds, crushed

2 cups buttermilk or milk

4 eggs

2 cups canned green enchilada sauce

SPANISH RICE

ᴥ Serves 4 ᴥ

Exactly what makes this rice Spanish has never been clear, but with this collection of tasty Tex-Mex ingredients, it is clear why it's such a delicious dish. It also easily becomes vegetarian if you omit the shredded meat and stock. Please note that rice prepared in the slow cooker will not retain the shape and individuality of each grain as it would in a rice cooker.

Preheat the broiler. Place the chiles, tomatoes, and onion skin side up on a baking sheet. Place under the broiler and grill for about 10 minutes, until the skins are blackened. Cover the vegetables with a damp kitchen towel and let rest for about 20 minutes. Peel off the chile and tomato skins or scrape them off using a paring knife. Slice the chiles into $1/4$-inch strips and coarsely chop the tomatoes, garlic, and onion.

Spread half of the shredded meat in a layer in the bottom of the slow cooker. Pour the rice on top of the meat. Spoon in a layer of the roasted chiles, tomatoes, and onion. Add the remaining meat and the rice. Spoon on the remaining chiles, tomatoes, and onion.

Combine the water or stock and salt in a small bowl and stir until the salt is dissolved. Pour into the cooker. Cover and cook on low for about 6 hours, until the rice is tender and the liquid has been absorbed.

About 15 minutes before serving, sprinkle the cheese over the top of the casserole. Serve hot sprinkled with parsley and a dollop of sour cream.

SUGGESTED BEVERAGE: A good Mexican beer or Mexican red wine. If you'd like a special treat and can find it, try Vino de Piedra, a superb blend of Cab and Tempranillo from the Guadalupe Valley's Casa de Piedra.

3 poblano chiles, halved, stemmed, and seeded

6 tomatoes, halved

3 cloves garlic

1 large white onion, cut into 6 pieces

$1^1/_2$ cups Shredded Beef (page 62)

2 cups uncooked rice

3 cups beef stock (page 91) or water

2 teaspoons salt

1 cup grated Monterey Jack or sharp cheddar cheese

$1/_2$ teaspoon dried Mexican oregano

Chopped fresh parsley or cilantro, for garnish

Sour cream, for garnish

CARIBBEAN PINK BEANS and SQUASH

—⌒ Serves 4 ⌒—

Although this dish has its origins in the Caribbean, it can be found in Florida and any other area in which there are Jamaican or Caribbean immigrants. It makes a hearty side and a good accompaniment to roasted pork loin.

Combine the beans, water, barley, tomatoes, bay leaf, garlic, allspice, ginger, brown sugar, and chile in the slow cooker. Cover and cook on low for 4 to 6 hours. Add the squash and sausage and continue to cook for 2 hours, until the flavors meld. (The squash and sausage can be added when you first put the dish on to cook, but I prefer the more distinctive shape and flavors that remain with the shorter cooking time.) Season to taste with salt.

Place a sauté pan over medium-high heat. Add the bacon and cook, turning, until crispy. Transfer to paper towels to drain, and then crumble.

Spoon the beans into bowls and serve hot, garnished with the bacon and green onions.

SUGGESTED BEVERAGE: A good Jamaican beer such as Red Stripe.

2 cups dried red or pink beans

4 cups chicken stock (page 91) or water

2 tablespoons barley

1 (14-ounce) can chopped tomatoes, undrained

1 bay leaf

6 cloves garlic

10 allspice berries, crushed

$1/2$ teaspoon ground ginger

1 tablespoon brown sugar

1 Scotch bonnet chile, stemmed, seeded, and finely chopped

1 butternut squash, peeled and cut into cubes

$1/2$ pound spicy sausage, cut into rounds

Salt

1 lean bacon slice

2 green onions, white and light green parts only, finely chopped, for garnish

STEWED TOMATOES

— Serves 4 —

In the South, a Blue Plate Special was historically a quick and inexpensive meal for travelers served on popular Blue Willow china. The term came into common usage in the early 1900s at diners, where it was used to refer to the special of the day. Serve stewed tomatoes as a side to your own Blue Plate Special, such as fried chicken or chicken-fried steak.

Place a large sauté pan over medium-high heat and add the butter. Add the celery and onion and sauté for about 5 minutes, until soft. Stir in the garlic, tomatoes, sugar, and allspice and cook for 10 minutes, until heated through.

Transfer the contents of the pan to the slow cooker. Cover and cook on low for about 4 hours, until the tomatoes have broken down. Just before serving, add the lemon juice and season to taste with salt and pepper.

SUGGESTED BEVERAGE: Since stewed tomatoes are likely to be a side dish, you're better off matching your drink with your main course.

1 tablespoon unsalted butter

4 celery stalks, cut into $^1/_2$-inch dice

1 yellow onion, cut into $^1/_2$-inch dice

2 cloves garlic, minced

8 large ripe tomatoes, cut into chunks

1 tablespoon dark brown sugar

Pinch of ground allspice

2 teaspoons freshly squeezed lemon juice

Salt and freshly ground black pepper

LIMA BEANS and HAM HOCKS

—⁊ Serves 4 ⁊—

Lima beans and ham hocks are true southern soul food. The beans supply protein and energy-rich carbohydrates, and the ham adds delicious flavor.

Place the lima beans in the slow cooker.

Place a sauté pan over medium-high heat and add the vegetable oil. Add the onion, celery, and carrots and sauté for about 10 minutes, until lightly browned.

Transfer the contents of the pan to the slow cooker and add the water and ham hock. Cover and cook on low for 5 to 7 hours. Remove the ham hock and strip it of as much fat as you can. Return the meat to the pot and continue to cook for 1 hour, until the beans are very tender. Season to taste with salt and pepper.

Serve hot, garnished with the parsley.

SUGGESTED BEVERAGE: A hearty red wine (commonly drunk with bean dishes in Italy and France) or a good beer.

1 pound dried lima beans, thoroughly rinsed

1 tablespoon vegetable oil

1 yellow onion, chopped

2 celery stalks, diced

2 small carrots, diced

8 cups chicken stock (page 91) or water

1 ham hock

Salt and freshly ground black pepper

1/4 cup chopped fresh parsley, for garnish

LOGANBERRY BARBECUE SAUCE

—⌁ Makes about 1 pint ⌁—

Whidbey Island in Washington's Puget Sound is one of the most beautiful places in the Pacific Northwest. At one time, the island was home to the world's largest loganberry farm. Loganberries can now be purchased fresh or frozen in many markets, but boysenberries or blackberries would work as well. The sauce is particularly good with chicken, duck, or game hens.

Place a large sauté pan over medium-high heat and add the oil. Add the onion and sauté for about 5 minutes, just until soft. Add the garlic and sauté for 2 minutes. Transfer the contents to the slow cooker and add the loganberry wine, vinegar, loganberries, brown sugar, Worcestershire sauce, and pepper flakes. Stir well. Cover and cook on low for 6 to 8 hours, until thickened. A few minutes before serving, stir in the lemon juice and salt to taste.

Tightly covered, the sauce will keep for 2 weeks in the refrigerator.

SUGGESTED BEVERAGE: Greenbank Farm Loganberry Wine, a good Pinot Noir, or any medium-bodied red wine with distinct berry aromas.

1 tablespoon vegetable oil

1/2 yellow onion, chopped

2 cloves garlic, minced

1/4 cup loganberry wine or Pinot Noir

1/4 cup apple cider vinegar

2 1/2 pounds frozen or fresh loganberries, boysenberries, or blackberries

1/4 cup packed brown sugar

1 tablespoon Worcestershire sauce

Pinch of red pepper flakes

Juice of 1 lemon

Salt

APRICOT PRESERVES

—⌁ Makes about 1 cup ⌁—

The slow cooker is an excellent tool for making small batches of jams and preserves—just enough for a week's worth of morning toast—without any fuss at all. You can use your stovetop recipes, just adjust for longer cooking times. Begin on low and end on high with the cover off, and plan on watching somewhat carefully for the last hour. Forsake the pectin and enjoy the spoonable texture of nothing but fruit.

Combine the apricots, juice, and zest, in a 2½- or 3-quart slow cooker. Cover and cook on low for about 4 hours, until thick and spoonable. Preserves will thicken as they cool, but if they need to thicken further, remove the lid, increase the heat to high, and cook for another hour. Refrigerate and use within one week.

8 ounces dried apricots

2 cups freshly squeezed orange juice

About 1 tablespoon grated orange zest

SOUR CHERRY CHUTNEY

— Makes about 1 cup —

This wonderful chutney can be used as an accompaniment for grilled lamb, rice pilaf, or even spicy pumpkin muffins.

Combine all the ingredients in a 2½- or 3-quart slow cooker. Cover and cook on low for about 4 hours. Uncover, increase the heat to high, and cook for 1 hour, until thick and spoonable. Refrigerate and use within one week.

8 ounces dried cherries

2 cups water

¼ cup dried currants

2 tablespoons apple cider vinegar

¼ to ½ cup packed brown sugar

½ teaspoon freshly grated peeled ginger

2 allspice berries, ground

MUSHROOM and ARTICHOKE RAGÙ

—◦ Serves 4 ◦—

This dish takes a bit more prep time than your average throw-everything-in-a-pot slow cooker recipe, but it's well worth it. This luscious ragù can be served as a side for grilled steak or lamb, as a topping for pasta or rice, or as an entrée with a green salad and crunchy bread.

Combine the flour and salt in a resealable plastic bag. Add the artichoke hearts and shake until evenly coated.

Place a large sauté pan over medium-high heat and add some of the oil and butter. Add the artichokes and sauté for about 15 minutes, until golden brown. Transfer to the slow cooker.

Heat more of the oil and butter in the pan and add the portobello, button, cremini, and mixed mushrooms in batches. Sauté for 10 minutes, until lightly golden. Transfer the mushrooms to the cooker and mix with the artichokes.

Heat the remaining oil and butter in the pan and add the shallots. Sauté for about 10 minutes, until browned. Add the port to the pan and scrape up any browned bits with a wooden spoon. Pour the liquid and the shallots into the slow cooker and add the thyme. Cover and cook on low for about 4 hours, until the flavors are blended. Season to taste with salt and pepper and serve warm.

SUGGESTED BEVERAGE: Something gutsy, like a New World–style Pinot from California's Santa Rita Hills. Even a nice Cab or Merlot from Washington State would work well.

1/2 cup all-purpose flour

1 teaspoon salt

1 (12-ounce) package good-quality frozen artichoke hearts, thawed

1/4 cup olive oil

4 tablespoons unsalted butter

1 pound portobello mushrooms, cut into large chunks

1 pound button mushrooms, trimmed and halved

1 pound cremini mushrooms, trimmed and halved

1 pound mixed shiitake, oyster, chanterelle, and morel mushrooms, trimmed and halved

4 shallots, finely minced

1/2 cup port, sherry, or hearty red wine

4 sprigs thyme

Freshly ground black pepper

New England Brown Bread

—⚬ Serves 4 ⚬—

Steaming bread in the slow cooker is a terrific, hassle-free way to bake bread of all kinds. Traditionally, the batter for this brown bread was poured into coffee cans and placed in deep kettles filled with water, then hung for hours over the fire to steam. Serve it with New England Baked Beans (opposite page) or toasted for breakfast with cream cheese.

Remove one end from two (1-pound) coffee cans. Clean and grease thoroughly.

In a large bowl, whisk together the flour, cornmeal, salt, baking soda, currants, cinnamon, and allspice, if desired. In a smaller bowl, whisk the wet ingredients together. Make a well in the center of the dry ingredients, then whisk in the wet ingredients until thoroughly incorporated.

Divide the batter evenly between the prepared coffee cans. The cans should be about two-thirds full to allow for expansion during cooking. Tightly cover the top of each can with aluminum foil.

Place the cans in the slow cooker and pour water halfway up their sides. Cover and cook on high for $2^1/2$ to 3 hours, until the tops of the loaves puff slightly and a knife or skewer inserted into the middle comes out clean.

Remove the coffee cans from the slow cooker and allow to cool for about 15 minutes. Turn the cans upside down and gently shake out the bread; it should slide out easily.

3 cups whole wheat flour

1 cup cornmeal

1 teaspoon salt

2 teaspoons baking soda

1 cup currants (optional)

$^1/_2$ teaspoon ground cinnamon (optional)

$^1/_2$ teaspoon ground allspice (optional)

2 eggs

$^2/_3$ cup molasses

2 cups buttermilk

$^1/_3$ cup honey

New England Baked Beans

—⌕ Serves 4 ⌕—

Caramelized winter fruits atop these beans make for a wonderful variation of this traditional New England side dish.

Place a sauté pan over medium-high heat. Add the bacon and cook, turning, until crispy. Transfer to paper towels to drain, and chop.

Place the beans in the slow cooker and add the bacon, water, cider, onion, molasses, maple syrup, ginger, mustard, and cloves. Cover and cook on low for 6 to 8 hours, until the beans are tender. Season to taste with salt.

Place a large sauté pan over medium-high heat and add the butter. Add the apples and pears and cook for about 10 minutes, until they begin to brown. Sprinkle with the brown sugar and cinnamon and sauté for about 5 minutes.

When the liquid is almost evaporated from the slow cooker, place the fruit mixture on top of the beans and continue cooking for about 40 minutes, until the flavors are melded.

Divide evenly among bowls and serve at once.

SUGGESTED BEVERAGE: A delicious hard cider from an artisan producer such as Rhyne Cyder in Sonoma County, or a fruity microbrew.

2 thick hickory-smoked bacon slices

1 pound dried white beans, thoroughly rinsed

4 cups water

2 cups apple cider or hard apple cider

1 yellow onion, finely chopped

$1/2$ cup molasses

$1/2$ cup maple syrup

$1/8$ teaspoon ground ginger

1 teaspoon dry mustard

$1/8$ teaspoon ground cloves

Salt

4 tablespoons unsalted butter

2 apples, cored, peeled, and sliced

2 pears, cored and sliced

$1/4$ cup brown sugar

$1/2$ teaspoon ground cinnamon

WILD RICE and BLACK WALNUT PILAF

—◦ Serves 4 ◦—

So-called wild rice is actually a grain that grows in the Great Lakes region and has been harvested by the Ojibway and Cree Indians for centuries. Because of how long it takes to cook, wild rice is perfect for the slow cooker. Black walnuts, native to the central and eastern United States, have a very different flavor than English walnuts, though the garden variety English walnut can be used in a pinch.

Place the rice in the slow cooker.

Place a large sauté pan over medium-high heat and add the butter. Add the onion, mushrooms, and celery and sauté for about 5 minutes, until soft. Transfer to the slow cooker and add the water and currants. Cover and cook on low for $2^{1}/_{2}$ to 3 hours, until the rice just starts to burst open. Do not overcook or the rice will get mushy. Season to taste with salt.

Preheat the oven to 350°F. Spread the walnuts in an even layer on a baking sheet. Cook for about 10 minutes, until toasted.

Divide the pilaf among plates and serve warm, garnished with the walnuts and green onions.

SUGGESTED BEVERAGE: A crisp, acidic, well-chilled Pinot Gris, Pinot Blanc, or even a lighter-style Pinot Noir.

1 cup wild rice, well rinsed

1 tablespoon unsalted butter

$^{1}/_{2}$ yellow onion, chopped

1 cup assorted fresh wild mushrooms, stemmed and sliced

2 celery stalks thinly sliced

3 cups chicken stock (page 91) or water

$^{1}/_{4}$ cup dried currants or dried cranberries

Salt

1 cup black walnuts, coarsely chopped

$^{1}/_{2}$ cup chopped green onions, green parts only, for garnish

Warm Corn Pudding

— Serves 4 —

The sugar in corn begins to turn to starch as soon as it is picked. So, to get the maximum flavor for your corn pudding, use very fresh corn, preferably picked the same day, or a high-quality frozen product. Serve alongside any kind of grilled meat, especially lamb, or with a simple salad for lunch.

Place a large sauté pan over medium-high heat and add the butter. Add the onion and sauté for about 7 minutes, until lightly browned. Add the corn kernels and mix well. Transfer to the slow cooker.

In a blender or with a whisk, beat together the eggs, milk, sugar, mustard, Tabasco sauce, and salt. Pour over the vegetables in the cooker. Cover and cook on low for 2 to $2^1/_2$ hours, until a knife inserted into the center comes out clean. Be careful not to overcook.

Allow the pudding to cool for at least 30 minutes before scooping into bowls. Garnish each portion with the chives and cheese and serve at once.

SUGGESTED BEVERAGE: A well-chilled Chenin Blanc or an un-oaked Chardonnay.

2 tablespoons unsalted butter

1 yellow onion, finely chopped

3 cups fresh or frozen corn kernels

4 eggs

2 cups low-fat milk, whole milk, or half-and-half

1 teaspoon sugar

1 teaspoon Dijon mustard

Few drops of Tabasco sauce

$^1/_2$ teaspoon salt

Chopped fresh chives, for garnish

Grated cheddar, for garnish

BRAISED ONIONS with RAISINS and ALMONDS

—◦ Serves 4 ◦—

Braised onions with raisins and almonds is a Spanish-inspired dish from the southwestern border of the United States. It makes a sweet topping for rice or side to any barbecued meat.

In a coffee mill or using a mortar and pestle, grind the cinnamon, cloves, and allspice to a fine powder. Place the spices and onions in the cooker and add the water or chicken stock.

Cook on low for 6 hours, or until onions are tender. Add the tomato sauce, salt, and raisins and cook for 30 minutes more. Top with the almonds and parsley and serve immediately.

SUGGESTED BEVERAGE: A Rueda verdejo, a fruity and fresh Spanish wine, like the one from Oro de Castilla, or a light-bodied Côtes du Rhône or pinot noir.

1 cinnamon stick

8 whole cloves

6 allspice berries

6 medium onions, any color, peeled and cut into quarters

1 cup chicken stock (page 91) or water

1 cup tomato sauce

1/2 teaspoon salt

1/2 cup golden raisins

1/4 cup slivered almonds, toasted, for garnish

1/2 cup chopped fresh parsley, for garnish

Desserts

Spicy Chocolate Truffles / 82

Coffee-Chocolate Pot de Crème / 84

Indian Pudding / 85

Apricot Gingerbread Upside-Down Cake / 86

Poached Pears in Cinnamon-Spice Sauce / 87

Georgia Peach Cobbler / 88

Spicy Chocolate Truffles

—⚬ Makes about 18 truffles ⚬—

The gentle heat supplied by the slow cooker is an effortless way to temper chocolate without having to use a double boiler, standing over the pot to keep careful watch. With the small amount of chocolate required, the recipe works better in a 3-quart slow cooker rather than a 5-quart, for better control over the melting process. The recipe can also be doubled for double the chocolate indulgence.

Combine the chocolate, cream, butter, and coffee in the slow cooker. Cover and cook on low for 40 to 60 minutes, until the chocolate melts. Stir once or twice during the cooking time, just to make sure that the chocolate does not stick to the bottom or sides of the crock. Whisk the mixture vigorously when it is nearly melted.

Pour the melted chocolate onto a plate or into a glass bowl and place in the refrigerator for between ½ and 1 hour, until it is hard enough to form into small balls.

Combine the cinnamon, cloves, and allspice in a coffee mill or using a mortar and pestle and grind them to a coarse powder. Transfer to a small bowl, add the cocoa powder, and mix thoroughly.

Line a baking sheet with aluminum foil. Using a spoon or mini ice cream scoop, scoop out spoonfuls of the chocolate mixture and roll with your hands into balls the size of walnuts. (This is a great job for kids. Just have plenty of paper towels on hand!) Roll the balls in the cocoa mixture and place them on the prepared baking sheet.

Place the truffles in the refrigerator for at least 4 hours or up to overnight. Sprinkle the truffles with the confectioners' sugar and allow to sit at room temperature for about 1 hour before serving.

SUGGESTED BEVERAGE: A good strong cup of espresso or a lovely sparkling wine from Gruet Winery in New Mexico.

16 ounces bittersweet chocolate or bittersweet chocolate chips

²/₃ cup heavy whipping cream

2 tablespoons unsalted butter

¹/₄ cup coffee beans, finely ground

2 cinnamon sticks

4 whole cloves

6 allspice berries

¹/₂ cup unsweetened cocoa powder

Confectioners' sugar, for powdering

Coffee-Chocolate Pot de Crème

—◦ Serves 4 ◦—

Making this rich, delicious dessert is a no-brainer in the slow cooker. Serve with freshly whipped cream.

Generously butter the slow cooker insert.

Combine all the ingredients in a blender and process until thoroughly mixed. Pour into the prepared slow cooker. Cover and cook on low for about 2½ hours, until a knife inserted into the center comes out clean. If the edges of the custard begin to puff, it's time to turn off the heat.

Turn off the cooker, remove the insert, and let the custard cool at room temperature for at least 1 hour. Place in the refrigerator and let cool for at least 4 hours before serving.

SUGGESTED BEVERAGE: A good cuppa Joe, or the Late Harvest White Riesling from Hogue Cellars in Prosser, Washington.

4 cups half-and-half

²/₃ cup sugar

¹/₄ cup good-quality instant espresso powder

¹/₂ teaspoon pure maple extract

2 tablespoons unsweetened cocoa powder

6 eggs

INDIAN PUDDING

—⌒ Serves 4 ⌒—

The name of this dessert or breakfast treat comes from colonial settlers in New England who substituted corn, or "Indian meal," to make English pudding when wheat flour was in short supply. The pudding is sublime when served with clotted cream, whipped cream, or vanilla ice cream.

Lightly grease the insert of a 2½- to 3-quart slow cooker. Combine all the ingredients in the cooker and whisk together thoroughly. Cover and cook on low for 4 to 5 hours, until set.

Allow to cool slightly, then spoon generous portions into bowls.

SUGGESTED BEVERAGE: A classic dessert wine such as a Canadian ice wine or one from the Greek Samos Co-op.

4 cups whole milk

½ cup heavy whipping cream or half-and-half

½ cup medium to coarse cornmeal

¼ cup molasses

3 tablespoons light or dark brown sugar

½ teaspoon ground cinnamon

½ teaspoon ground nutmeg or ground ginger

Pinch of salt

1 teaspoon pure vanilla extract

2 eggs

3 tablespoons unsalted butter (optional)

APRICOT GINGERBREAD UPSIDE-DOWN CAKE

—◦ Serves 6 ◦—

This is a flavorful variation on the timeless pineapple upside-down cake. Here dried apricots are used, but the cake can be made with a variety of dried or preserved fruits with equally good results. It's excellent topped with a dollop of whipped cream, ice cream, or creamy Greek-style yogurt.

In a bowl, combine the dried apricots with the $^1/_2$ cup water or apple juice and soak overnight.

Place the butter, $^1/_2$ cup of the brown sugar, and the apricots in the slow cooker and cook on high until the butter melts and the sugar dissolves. Stir to coat the apricots. Spread the coated apricots evenly over the bottom of the cooker.

In a large bowl, beat together the oil, remaining 1 cup brown sugar, and the egg until thoroughly mixed. Beat in the molasses and the $^1/_2$ cup warm water. Add the flour, baking soda, salt, and ginger and mix well. Gently pour the batter over the apricots and spread evenly.

Cook on high for about $2^1/_2$ hours, or until a knife or skewer inserted in the center of the cake comes out clean. Halfway through the cooking, using pot holders, carefully lift the insert out of the slow cooker and turn it around to ensure even cooking.

To unmold the cake, place a large plate over the cooker insert. Tightly gripping them together with pot holders, invert the insert over the plate. The cake should slip out easily. Scoop into bowls and serve immediately.

SUGGESTED BEVERAGE: A Canadian ice wine such as Gray Monk from the Okanagan Valley, which has a lovely note of apricot.

2 cups dried apricots

$^1/_2$ cup water or apple juice

$^1/_4$ cup unsalted butter

$1^1/_2$ cups brown sugar

$^1/_2$ cup vegetable oil

1 large egg

$^1/_2$ cup molasses

$^1/_2$ cup warm water

2 cups all-purpose flour

2 teaspoons baking soda

$^1/_2$ teaspoon salt

1 tablespoon ground ginger

Poached Pears in Cinnamon-Spice Sauce

↦ Serves 4 ↤

These poached pears are especially luscious with their Pacific Rim accent. Locally grown, in-season, organic pears are far superior for this slow-cooked dessert than store-bought fruit shipped from far away.

Add the water, cinnamon, allspice, ginger, and sugar to the slow cooker and cook on high for 1 hour.

Remove and discard the spices and ginger. Place the pear halves in the slow cooker and cook on low for 4 hours, until the pears are just tender when pierced with a fork. Turn carefully once or twice during the cooking to ensure the flavors are evenly distributed.

To serve, place the pears on a serving platter or individual plates and spoon the poaching liquid over the top. Serve piping hot or chilled.

SUGGESTED BEVERAGE: Try a Zinfandel port with this.

3 cups water

2 cinnamon sticks

2 allspice berries

One 1-inch piece fresh ginger, peeled and thinly sliced

1 2/3 cup sugar

4 very firm pears, sliced in half lengthwise and seeded

GEORGIA PEACH COBBLER

—◦ Serves 4 ◦—

Although native to China, peaches have been grown in Georgia since breeders began developing new varieties during the early 1900s. And while pecans are native to Texas, today they too are grown commercially in Georgia. This is a simple cobbler that requires little attention after the ingredients have been assembled and put in to cook, and it tastes simply delicious.

Combine the peaches, cinnamon, and granulated sugar in a large bowl and toss to coat evenly. Transfer to the slow cooker.

Combine the flour, oats, brown sugar, and butter in the bowl of a food processor and pulse until the mixture is the consistency of coarse cornmeal. Add the pecans and stir in with a spoon. Spread the crumble evenly over the peaches.

Cover and cook on high for about 2 hours, until the peaches are tender, the juices are bubbling around the sides, and the topping is cooked through.

SUGGESTED BEVERAGE: A good dessert wine.

6 large peaches (about 2 1/2 pounds), peeled and sliced

2 teaspoons ground cinnamon

1/4 cup granulated sugar

1/4 cup all-purpose flour

3/4 cup rolled oats

1/2 cup packed brown sugar

6 tablespoons unsalted butter

1 cup pecans, coarsely chopped

STOCKS

Stock made on the low setting of your slow cooker will be clearer than one that has been brought to a boil on the stovetop. It's cheaper to make stock than to buy it, and it tastes a whole lot better. And homemade stock can be refrigerated overnight so that most of the congealed fat can be removed the next day.

I always keep bags of frozen poultry, meat, and fish bones in the freezer. Each time I have leftover parts from a recipe, I toss them into the bag, and when I have a sufficient amount of bones, I make a stock. And I always use organic meats, poultry, fish, and vegetables to avoid ingesting concentrations of pesticides.

Chicken or Turkey Stock

2¹/₂ pounds chicken or turkey necks, backs, and giblets

8 cups water

Fish Stock

2 tablespoons olive oil

2 medium yellow onions, peeled and coarsely chopped

1 pound fish heads and bones

1 celery stalk, cut into chunks

2 sprigs fresh thyme

2 whole garlic cloves, peeled

8 cups water

Meat Stock

1 large onion, peeled and coarsely chopped

1 pound short ribs or bones

1 celery stalk, cut in chunks

1 large carrot, cut in chunks

1 small bunch parsley

4 whole garlic cloves, peeled

For each stock, combine all ingredients in the slow cooker. Cover and cook on low for 8 hours, until all the meat has fallen off the bones.

Strain the stock through a medium-meshed sieve into a bowl. Refrigerate overnight, then skim off the congealed fat the next day. Use immediately, refrigerate for up to 3 days, or freeze for up to 3 months.

Index

Also available from the Gourmet series

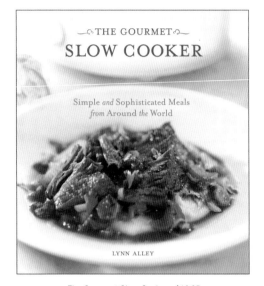

The Gourmet Slow Cooker • $18.95
ISBN-13: 978-1-58008-489-5 • ISBN-10: 1-58008-489-3
100,000 copies sold

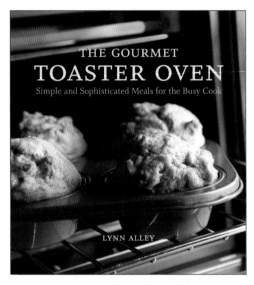

The Gourmet Toaster Oven • $18.95
ISBN-13: 978-1-58008- 659-2 • ISBN-10: 1-58008-659-4

The Gourmet Potluck • $18.95
ISBN-13: 978-1-58008-741-4 • ISBN-10: 1-58008-741-8